TEACHER'S GUIDE FOR

Rufus Rides a Catfish

Copyright © 2021 Charles B. Roegiers

Illustrated by Priscilla Patterson

All rights reserved. This includes the right to reproduce any portion of this book in any form.

LCCN: 2019917178

Rufus Rides a Catfish: First Hardcover Edition (2019)
ISBN: 978-1-7321976-4-0
Rufus Rides a Catfish: First Softcover Edition (2020)
ISBN: 978-1-7321976-7-1

Teachers Guide　　　　　　　　　　　　ISBN-978-1-952493-13-3
　　　　　　Student Booklets (2021)

Fable 1:	Rufus Rides a Catfish:	ISBN 978-1-952493-04-1
Fable 2:	Trip and the Cottonwood:	ISBN 978-1-952493-03-4
Fable 3:	Hic the Pig:	ISBN 978-1-952493-05-8
Fable 4:	The Tragic Tale of Limpin' Libby:	ISBN 978-1-952493-06-5
Fable 5:	Ellie's Big Day:	ISBN 978-1-952493-07-2
Fable 6:	Red and Blue (Part 1):	ISBN 978-1-952493-08-9
Fable 7:	Cecil Redner's Pumpkin Patch:	ISBN 978-1-952493-09-6
Fable 8:	The Golden Lamb:	ISBN 978-1-952493-10-2
Fable 9:	Red and Blue (Part 2):	ISBN 9781--952493-11-9
Fable 10:	The Mysterious Case of the Disappearing Ducklings	ISBN 978-1-952493-12-6

Young Adult Fiction

Jujapa Press, LLC, Hansville WA

Jujapapress@aol.com

Distributed by Ingram Spark

For My Father

Preface

Fables are designed to teach. But more than just that, fables offer an impetus for evocative discussion and an opportunity for the rational exchange of ideas.

The fables from the "Rufus Rides a Catfish" collection were written to challenge young minds in a fun and exciting way. Set in the 1970's American heartland, they tackle a wide spectrum of topics, including some very difficult situations, interpersonal and societal.

As with the subject matter, the vocabulary is not "dumbed down." Rather, it seeks to expand the linguistic tools of its readers. At the end of each fable, a Student Worksheet provides a list of vocabulary words used in that particular story that students may look up and define in their own words. This Teacher's Guide contains these lists along with suggested definitions.

The students are then encouraged to discuss the moral of the fable with help from the teacher. The author has provided some minimal guidance in that arena as well.

Finally, a short series of thought-provoking questions are put to the readers. Some ask for opinion, some encourage discussion, and some are cell phone look-ups! Again, intellectual discussion is encouraged and this Teacher's Guide provides some possible thoughts to facilitate those discussions in an engaging way.

In addition to the worksheets, these fables offer a look into what rural life was like in the mid to late twentieth century. Historical facts, social mores, geographical trivia, and even spiritual diversity are all couched in an environment with talking animals and their people. The individual characteristics of each person and animal are worth exploring as well. For example, Rufus the Cat is noble and valiant, and perhaps a bit delusional. What is the primary trait of Lulu the Labrador?

The book-set is a collaborative labor of love between father and son, and that duality is represented throughout the stories by pairings of names, places, and circumstances. It may be fun to look for those pairings. Additionally, adjectives and metaphors used in each story are often couched in the theme of that particular fable. More thought-provoking and educational conversation!

Enjoy the experience!

Rufus Rides a Catfish
Fable #1 – Teacher's Guide

Vocabulary Words

1. Transverse. Adjective – situated or extending across something

2. Stoic. Adjective – able to endure hardship without showing emotion

3. Parlance. Noun – a particular way of speaking

4. Entrepreneur. Noun – an enterprising business person

5. Palatable. Adjective – able to be tasted

6. Intrepid. Adjective – fearless, adventurous

7. Indiscriminately. Adverb – in a random manner

8. Meander. Verb – wander aimlessly

9. Tributary. Noun – a river or stream flowing into a larger body of water

10. Piscatorial. Adjective – having to do with fish or fishing

11. Transcendental. Adjective – relating to a spiritual or nonphysical realm

12. Tumultuous. Adjective – loud, confusing, excited

Class Discussion: What does the moral mean to you in your own words?

Suggestion: The kindness exhibited by old Marcus Anderson and the boys in the boat, who saved Rufus, affected little Ree-Ree so strongly that she lovingly named her two sons after these men. This simple act undoubtedly served as a moral "compass" in her life and she passed that philosophy along to her own children, long after old Marcus had died.

Questions

1. What does the author mean, on page 14, by "a purely democratic" vote?

"Purely democratic," in this usage, refers to the dictionary definition and not a political party. Direct democracy is a system where people vote directly, in other words, "majority rules." As the kids would say, "Three against one; we're right!"

2. At the river, Trip figured that four hooks in the water, instead of three, increased the odds of catching a fish by one third … or was it one fourth? Which is correct? (p. 15)

*It **increases** their odds by one third. The word "increases" is the key.*

3. Is the enormous catfish described on page 19 still the largest on record?

Cell phone look up!

4. Who does your dog think you are? (p. 18)

Imagine!

5. On page 22, Rufus dug eighteen claws into the fish! Why not twenty … or sixteen?

Oddly enough, cats have five toes on each of their front paws, but only four on each of their rear paws!

6. Marcus Anderson is described, on page 26, as a sage, old farmer? In this context, what is the meaning of the word "sage?"

Here, it is used as an adjective to describe profound wisdom.

Trip and the Cottonwood
Fable #2 – Teacher's Guide

Vocabulary Words

1. Nomenclature. Noun – relating to the naming of things

2. Tenuous. Adjective – very weak or slight

3. Belied. Verb – to give a false impression of something

4. Tête-à-tête. Noun – a private conversation between two people

5. Manic. Adjective – related to the noun, mania – crazy, deranged, frantic

6. Arduous. Adjective – requiring hard work; difficult and tiring

7. Inroads. Noun – progress

8. Epithet. Noun – nickname, label

9. Myopia. Noun – nearsightedness, lack of imagination

10. Exponentially. Noun – (with reference to an increase) more and more rapidly

11. Enigmatically. Adverb – mysteriously

12. Inexorable. Adjective – impossible to stop

Class Discussion: What does the moral mean to you in your own words?

Suggestion: When we join forces with others to overcome obstacles, we build strong relationships with our fellow combatants. These experiences, especially the bold and outlandish, are quite fun to recount when "spinning a yarn" later in life. It is especially sweet when shared with family. With this in mind, perhaps we should value adversity more!

Questions

1. Briefly describe the difference between "emigrate" and "immigrate." (page 3)

*"Emigrate" means to **leave** one's home country.*
*"Immigrate" is when one **comes** to another country to live.*

2. What would make Bud's "vast array of nicknames," as described on page 5, counterintuitive?

If they went against common-sense, or intuition.
Bud did not exhibit "copious care for details!"

3. Why would Lulu care, on page 9, if Bud was "the *alpha* in this pack?"
What "pack?"

Here, the word "pack" is used, from a dog's perspective, to represent the family. The strongest dog in a pack is often referred to as the "alpha." As head of the household, or family, Lulu would see Bud as the "alpha" in this "pack."

4. On page 23, the boys are said to have "jury-rigged" a cable around the core of the tree. What is the historical origin of that term?

Cell phone lookup! Discuss!
See "[jury mast](#)," and the Old French term ajurie, meaning "help."

5. What does the author mean, on page 31, when he describes "a maelstrom of painful switches?"

In past times, when a youngster misbehaved badly, and was to be punished, parents would often tell the youngster to "go pick out a switch" or a thin, flexible branch, that would then be used to punish the child. The conventional wisdom of the time suggested that the psychological torment of having to select the method of one's own demise added to the educational experience. Here, Trip and Lulu are flogged by the multitude of "switch-like" branches from the top of the falling tree!

Hic the Pig
Fable #3 – Teacher's Guide

Vocabulary Words

1. Circumnavigate. Verb – go around or avoid (an obstacle)

2. Moniker. Noun – a name

3. Continence. Noun – regarding the control of one's bowels or bladder

4. Conundrum. Noun – a riddle, puzzle or difficult question; a mystery

5. Haggle. Verb – to dispute or bargain persistently, especially over price

6. Drove (of pigs). Noun – a group of pigs

7. Perennial. Adjective – enduring or, in this case, continually recurring

8. Misogynistic. Adjective – prejudiced against women

9. Apex. Noun – the top

10. Oblige. Verb – do as someone asks in order to help or please them

11. Addled. Adjective – unable to think clearly; confused

12. Affable. Adjective – friendly and good-natured

Class Discussion: What does the moral mean to you in your own words?

Suggestion: This is a play on the adage, "Well-behaved women rarely make history." Think of the spectacular people in your life. How many of them would you describe as "normal" or as "a conformist?" Sometimes, being truly remarkable requires peculiar behavior!

Questions

1. Were scientists really predicting an Ice Age in the 1970s? (page 5)

Yes! Guessing the weather is hard, and sometimes controversial!

2. The Roegiers family had a special ring on their "party line" (page 7) to let them know that the call was for them. What is a party line?

In earlier times, telephone lines were often shared with other families, or "parties." In the cities, people could pay extra for a private line, an option not available for country folk. Sometimes, people would listen in on the private conversations of their neighbors! Can you imagine?

3. On page 23, Trip "spoke with regard to the *con*tent rather than the *in*tent of his mother's statement." What does this oddly-worded sentence mean?

*Trip took her words literally. Pigs are smart, so maybe they CAN be house-broken. Rosie just wanted the pig **OUT** of the house!*

4. A single word appears at the top of page 28, "détente." In this context, what does it mean?

"Détente" usually refers to relaxing tension between countries, but here, Ellie swooped in and snatched the piglet's bottle away from Duna, ending his argument with Ree-Ree.

5. What were the names of the two pigs who taunted Hic at the fair, and what is the significance of their names? (page 32)

"Patty" and "Linc" (short for Lincoln). Patties and links are types of sausage.

6. Why is a pig's tail curly?

Cell phone lookup! Discuss!

The Tragic Tale of Limpin' Libby
Fable #4 – Teacher's Guide

Vocabulary Words

1. Flaxen. Adjective – pale yellow, straw-like color

2. Mores, (Social). Noun – customs, the normal way of doing things

3. Octogenarian. Noun – a person who is between 80 and 89 years old

4. Coquettish. Adjective – playfully flirtatious behavior

5. Gilded. Adjective – covered with a thin layer of gold or gold coloring

6. Cathartic. Adjective – providing a relief of psychological stress

7. Swaddled. Verb – wrapped in cloth (like a baby)

8. Cliché. Noun – an overused or predictable phrase

9. Myriad. Adjective – a whole bunch of something

10. Jocularity. Noun – sense of humor

11. Carcass. Noun – the dead body of an animal

12. Stealthy. Adjective – sneaky, covert

Class Discussion: What does the moral mean to you in your own words?

Suggestion: Since the meaning of this moral is fairly straight-forward, try discussing the two types of motherly love displayed in this story. First, was the love of old Limpin' Libby, the three-legged mama cat, as she was forced to make the terrible choice to save only one kitten as her strength failed her. Second was Rosie's very personal struggle to understand why another mother (the cat) would abandon her offspring when they were threatened.

Questions

1. On page 3, the author accuses Bud of bald-faced bribery. Describe the history and meaning of the term "bald-faced."

*The expression comes from a time when most men wore facial hair and being bare-faced, or "bald-faced" was considered bold. The original term was "bald-faced lie" ("**bold**-faced" is now acceptable as well), so the author may have been implying that Bud was not being completely honest when he promised that the kids could each get a new pet when the family moved to the country!*

2. Bud is said to be "a big hit with *'le femme gériatrique'* set" on page 6. What does that mean?

"Le femme gériatrique" (French) translates literally to "the geriatric woman" or "the old woman." Old ladies love Bud.

3. What is a bull rake? (page 22)

Cell phone lookup! Discuss!

Here's a hint: this bull rake has nothing to do with clams!

4. Why did the author choose to have Dawn Marie curse when the skunk was killed? (page 48)

Little Dawn Marie was very personally invested in the lives of the four kittens. When she saw the skunk responsible for killing them, she felt an overpowering vengeful rage. The author chose to express her feelings this way to demonstrate the depth of her anger and her loss of control over it. Here, it is also used as a literary tool to provide some much needed comic relief in a very dark situation.

5. Chapter 21 is named "Requiem and Renaissance." Explain, in your own words, the meaning and significance of this title.

Requiem is a Mass for the dead. Renaissance literally means rebirth (French). Here, the two terms symbolize our sorrow over the deaths of the innocent cats and the hope of new life as baby Rufus joins the family.

Ellie's Big Day
Fable #5 – Teacher's Guide

Vocabulary Words

1. Undeterred. Adjective – continuing on, despite obstacles or hardship

2. Indiscriminate. Adjective – done randomly or without much thought

3. Malice. Noun – ill will, evil intentions

4. Naiveté. Noun – innocence, lack of experience

5. Per se. Adverb – in and of itself, intrinsically

6. Discernment. Noun – ability to judge well or make good decisions

7. Faux pas. Noun – a social blunder, embarrassing, French: literally, "false step"

8. Bona-Fide. Adjective – genuine, real, Latin: literally, "with good faith"

9. Antipathy. Noun – a deeply rooted feeling of dislike and mustrust

10. Cantankerous. Adjective – grumpy, bad-tempered, argumentative

11. Covenant. Noun – contract, agreement, promise

12. Hubris. Noun – excessive pride or self-confidence

Class Discussion: What does the moral mean to you in your own words?

Suggestion: This story explores both humility and optimism. Ellie exaggerated the quality and temperament of her party pony and was taught a lesson in humility. As she sat in that mud puddle in front of her party guests, she learned from her mistake and optimistically took a new direction in her life.

Questions

1. On page 8, Popeye the horse appears to be drunk on fermented apples. Is this a real things? If so, what happened?

Fermented apples react with the stomach acid in horses and other animals, converting to ethanol. We laugh, but ethanol poisoning can be very serious.

2. On page 22, Rosie told the story of one of her childhood neighbors dying from getting kicked in the chest by a horse. What happened to the poor guy?

Cell phone lookup! Discuss!
A severe blow to the chest could lead to death from any of a number of injuries, but a class discussion on safety and good judgment may save a life!

3. What is Hades? (page 26)

Colloquially, it is synonymous with Hell. Literally, Hades (hay'dees) was the name of the mythical Greek god of the underworld. Sending someone to Hades is the equivalent of sending them to the devil! Very rude!

4. During the pony rides, Trip refers to the horse as retarded. Though it was very commonly used without malice in 1974, its use is frowned upon today. What is the literal meaning of that word and why is it now considered controversial?

Literally, it simply means "slow." This is a marvelous opportunity for a carefully guided discussion about how word meanings change over time (and why) and how difficult it is to judge the past through the eyes of the present.

5. Who is Sweeney Todd? (page 40)

A fictional character, he was an evil barber in old London who murdered his customers and baked their remains into pies and then sold those pies to other customers who relished them!

6. If you could speak to anyone in history who has passed on, who would you choose? Why?

Keep it light!

Red & Blue (Part 1)
Fable #6 – Teacher's Guide

Vocabulary Words

1. Motif. Noun – (in literature) a distinctive theme or idea

2. Disconcerting. Adjective – unsettling or upsetting

3. Tenacious. Adjective – keeping a firm grip, determined

4. Devious. Adjective – underhanded, unscrupulous

5. Perfunctory. Adjective – done with little thought or effort

6. Cowackellak. Noun – mythical vital organ in sub-intelligent bovine

7. Rectitude. Noun – righteousness, moral correctness

8. Fray. Noun – a battle or fight

9. Boisterous. Adjective – noisy, energetic, rowdy

10. Piqued. Verb – stimulated

11. Surname. Noun – someone's last name

12. Beget. Verb – give rise to; bring about

Class Discussion: What does the moral mean to you in your own words?

Suggestion: This moral is a bit deeper than one would assume at first reading. Two things:
 1. It is a clever way to say, "Stay tuned for Part 2!"

 2. The deeper meaning – it is difficult to accurately understand a topic without all the facts. Be patient. Be thorough.

Questions

1. On page 5, Rufus says *"Bakayarō"* in frustration when Lulu interrupts the newcomer in-briefing. What does it mean?

Cell phone lookup! "Bakayarō" – the Japanese equivalent of "moron." We will learn more of Rufus' knowledge of Japanese in a later chapter. Foreshadowing!

2. What is the origin of the term "polka-dot?" (page 6)

In the late 1800s, when polka music was all the rage in Germany, this type of spotted material became popular on ladies' dresses worn to dances!

3. Explain Raymond Hill's math at the bottom of page 13.

The cost of Bud's bear claw and coffee went up from ninety-five cents to $1.05, a ten cent price hike. Ray quickly figured that one dollar covered the ten cent difference for ten weeks, or two and a half months! All too simple for a guy like Ray!

4. What were Lewis and Clark (page 23) attempting to discover in their 1805 expedition? Who sent them on their mission?

Among other things, they hoped to find a water route across the continental U.S. for the purposes of commerce, exploration, and expansion. The expedition was commissioned by President Thomas Jefferson.

5. Rosie asks Bud on page 32, "What on earth would two steers be doing in a circus?" What was Bud's reply?

"I dunno. Maybe they needed the milk."

6. Who is the real-life inspiration for the made up animal trainer in Bud's fantastic story, Üster Glüster-Williams?

Gunther Gebel-Williams – arguably the greatest circus animal trainer of all time!

Cecil Redner's Pumpkin Patch
Fable #7 – Teacher's Guide

Vocabulary Words

1. Continuity. Noun – the constant nature of an object or practice over time

2. Churlish. Adjective – rude, ill-mannered, impolite

3. Annunciatory. Adjective (?) – a playful variation of the word Annunciation, to announce

4. Indignantly. Adverb – showing annoyance or anger

5. Disparate. Adjective – fundamentally different

6. Mollified. Verb – reducing the anger or annoyance of someone; placate, pacify

7. Billy Club. Noun – a short stick used by police for self-defense when necessary

8. Din. Noun – a loud, unpleasant, prolonged noise

9. Valiant. Adjective – courageous, brave

10. Apoplectic. Adjective – so overcome with emotion (usually anger) that one can almost not even communicate

11. Visage. Noun – the face of a humanoid

12. Comeuppance. Noun – a well-earned punishment or consequence

Class Discussion: What does the moral mean to you in your own words? Do you have an illustration from your own family?

Suggestion: The lesson here is to not be so set in your own one-sided opinion that you disregard the opposing viewpoint. Be open-minded. You may learn something!

Questions

1. What is the origin of the expression "dog days?" (page 5)

It comes from ancient Greek mythology. Late summer is the time of year when the "dog star," Sirius, rises just before the sun. It has nothing to do with heat. After all, it's winter in the southern hemisphere!

2. The ornery old ewe had a funny name (page 5). After whom was she named and why?

She was named Circe, after the Greek witch, because of her foul temperament and bad manners. Greek again? Yep. We're building up to something.

3. What is the "right of parlay?" (page 8)

In the pirate code, it was allegedly used to call a truce in order to communicate peacefully with someone who might ordinarily be one's enemy. The pirate code was supposedly very real. As to its content, well, that's the stuff of the movies.

4. On page 15, what does Rufus discover that "could change everything?"

Rufus discovers that Lulu will obediently follow simple commands, regardless of their source!

5. The word "Daibutsu" is capitalized on page 17. Why?

Out of the author's deep respect for Japanese culture. The Daibutsu is one of any number of giant Buddha statues, often found on sacred, temple grounds throughout the country of Japan.

6. What do you think really happened in Cecil Redner's Pumpkin Patch?

Some clues are there, but the author intentionally leaves the question unanswered. The fable is about open communication with others, even when you do not know.

The Golden Lamb
Fable #8 – Teacher's Guide

Vocabulary Words

1. Raucous. Adjective – rowdy, making a loud, annoying noise

2. Confab. Noun – an informal, private conversation or meeting

3. Corollary. Noun – an idea that stems from and amends a previous, proven idea

4. Derivation. Noun – an idea that comes from (is *derived* from) another source

5. Crux. Noun – a decisive point in an issue, i.e. *crossroads* or *fork in the road*

6. Rhetorical. Adjective – relating to the art of rhetoric; persuasive speech

7. Double Entendre. Noun – a phrase with two possible meanings

8. Dilapidated. Adjective – a state of disrepair, broken down, shabby

9. Conjure. Verb – (in this story) call to mind, imagine

10. Furrowed. Adjective – (on a forehead) marked with lines or wrinkles

11. Smugly. Adverb – done in a way that shows excessive pride in oneself

12. Bluff. Noun – (in this story) a long cliff or ridge

Class Discussion: Why do you believe the author offered no moral for this story?

Suggestion: A moral is a life-lesson based on a story or experience. Marilyn was a real person and family friend of the author. Like many other women, including Bud's mother, Marilyn tragically lost her life to this disease. Tragedy begets no life-lesson beyond how to survive the loss of a loved one. This story ended with the shocking revelation that Marilyn did not survive. It did not explore that aspect of the grief process and therefore, in the author's personal opinion, did not deserve a moral.

Questions

1. On page 3, Ray Hill says that he might give the President a few pointers. Who was President of the United States in the fall of 1974?

Gerald R. Ford was President.
Richard M. Nixon resigned on August 9, 1974, only a few weeks earlier!

2. When Bud plays along with the kids on page 18, he claims to be Davy Jones and threatens to release the Kraken. Who is Davy Jones, and what is "the Kraken?"

"Davy Jones' Locker" is an old nautical metaphor for the bottom of the sea. Sailors do not want to visit Davy Jones! The Kraken is a mythical sea monster that attacks ships at sea, sending their crews to Davy Jones' Locker.
Rosie was NOT flattered when Bud wove her into the game as the Kraken!

3. Rufus exclaims, *"by Poseidon's beard!"* when speaking to Hic the Pig on page 26. Why did the author choose this exclamation in this particular story?

Poseidon is the Greek god of the sea. This story contains both Greek and nautical themes. Rufus must have understood this.

4. What and where was El Dorado (page 46)?

Many stories exist, but one story says that 16th Century Spanish explorers heard tales that El Dorado (literally, "the golden one") was a golden city in the Andes Mountains of the country now called Columbia, South America.

5. Can any breed of sheep fly?

Nope. Sorry, Duna. No sheep can fly.

6. What disease afflicted Marilyn Hill?

Breast Cancer.

Red & Blue (Part 2)
Fable #9 – Teacher's Guide

Vocabulary Words

1. Ominous. Adjective – the feeling that something bad is about to happen

2. Epiphany. Noun – a sudden moment of mental clarity or insight

3. Dew Claw. Noun – a vestigial digit on animals, often higher than other digits

4. Coveted. Adjective – highly desired

5. Rendezvous. Noun – a meeting, often between two people

6. Emaciated. Adjective – unusually thin and weak, often from lack of food

7. Faux. Adjective – made in imitation (i.e. faux pearls), fake

8. Layperson. Noun – a person without special training or knowledge of a subject

9. Surreptitiously. Adverb – secretively, sneaky

10. Laissez-Faire. Noun – an attitude of "letting things happen as they will"

11. Denizens. Noun – residents, occupants

12. Hypotheses. Noun (plural) – an educated guess; a proposed explanation

Class Discussion: What does the moral mean to you in your own words?

Suggestion: This is another lesson in humility. We have all met "Mr. (or Ms.) Know-it-all" and have found them to be annoying or off-putting. The two axioms, "ignorance is bliss" and "knowledge is power" both have merit and are true to a point. However, only through continued study do we learn and gain wisdom. That's why we go to school! This moral suggests that the first step in attaining wisdom is to have the humility to admit that you do ***not*** know something.

Questions

1. Do *you* agree that "participation trophies" mean nothing? (page 13) Why or why not?

Class Discussion – One opinion: once the recipient realizes that the praise he or she received is hollow, or unearned, they will feel no self-pride or sense of accomplishment. They may even learn to distrust the giver of such praise.

2. Blue seems terrified of the "long-noses."
Who are the long-noses and why is he frightened of them?

The "long-noses" are elephants. We are not sure why Blue is so terrified, aside from his assumption that they want to "inject him." But perhaps he believes that they hold him accountable for the "Great Brown Cow Clown Down Wiener-town disaster of 1973!"

3. On page 17, the BB pistol is referred to as Mark Wayne's "pièce de résistance." What does that mean?

Pièce de résistance (French) means "piece with resilience, strength, or staying power." We understand it to mean "masterpiece."

4. What was Woodstock (page 21)? Describe, in your own words, the facial expression that might have been worn by the "guy who had to clean up" after it.

Cell phone lookup! Discuss! Have fun with this. There is no wrong answer!

5. What did Ellie bring out to Trip and Ree-Ree (page 28) after the cattle judge made his announcement? Why?

She brought them two white paper napkins because white ribbons were so rare in cattle-showing contests that they didn't even have any at the judging table!

6. Why had Rufus never heard Hic laugh before? (page 37)

Because Hic (according to Hic) had never been so hilarious before.

The Mysterious Case of the Disappearing Ducklings
Fable #10 – Teacher's Guide

Vocabulary Words

1. Lexicon. Noun – vocabulary, the entire verbal language of a society or culture

2. Irrefutable. Adjective – impossible to deny or disprove

3. Magnanimously. Adverb – in a generous or charitable manner

4. Ambience. Noun – the atmosphere, aura, or "feeling" of a place

5. Congenial. Adjective – pleasant, agreeable

6. Pumpernickel. Noun – a type of thick, dark rye bread. "A ridiculous word, of course," according to Popeye.

7. Solfège. Noun – a style of teaching music using syllables, i.e. do, re, mi, etc.

8. Convergence. Noun – the coming together of different elements

9. Laden. Adjective – weighed down, loaded heavily

10. Mortified. Verb – embarrassed to death ("mort" Latin), figuratively

11. Exasperation. Noun – a feeling of intense irritation and annoyance

12. Whence. Adverb – an old way of saying "from where" or "from which"

Class Discussion: What does the moral mean to you in your own words?

Suggestion: The word "family" is enormous. It definitely can be defined as "people who are related to each other by blood," but it can also mean something more. Help the students explore the expanded definition of this powerful concept. You may wish to ask if some of them can share an example, in their own family history, of someone who is (or was) not a blood relation, but was nonetheless considered to be part of *their* "family."

Questions

1. Most people of a certain age know what it means to "sit on the hump" (page 6) in a car. What does that mean, and have *you* ever had to "sit on the hump?"

Older cars with Rear Wheel Drive had a "transmission tunnel" under the car for the linkage between the motor and the rear wheels. Newer cars with Front Wheel Drive use the same concept for the exhaust system. The bulging tunnel takes up space on the floor where your feet should go and is NOT a great place to sit!

2. According to Rufus, (page 17) what are the first words on the path to wisdom? Do those words sound familiar? Why or why not?

The words are, "I do NOT know." They should sound familiar. They are a distilled version of the moral from Fable #9, "Red & Blue (Part 2)."

3. What was the "inside joke" (page 25) shared between Belle and Rufus?

In Fable #8, "The Golden Lamb," Belle and Rufus had a friendly discussion, joking that listening to PBS made one smarter!

4. Given the details in the first paragraph on page 38, can you sing Hic's lullaby?

Give it a try! If you have a piano keyboard, "B, D, G" ascending!

5. On page 44, Rufus talks to the kitten about the "warrior class." To whom does this metaphor refer? What does he mean when he says, *"When facing a common foe, these dissenters can become worthy and powerful allies."*?

The metaphor expresses the author's deep respect and gratitude for members of the military, police force, and firefighters. The second sentence hearkens back to 9/11/2001, when political parties stopped bickering for a few weeks and joined forces. Just because someone disagrees with you does not make them your enemy!

6. Rufus tells Popeye (p. 47) "I shall have to call you Troy from now on." Why?

He is referring to the Trojan Horse used by the Greeks to covertly sneak into the city of Troy. Perhaps Popeye's pretending to be asleep reminded him of this story!

www.ingramcontent.com/pod-product-compliance
Lightning Source LLC
Chambersburg PA
CBHW081800100526
44592CB00015B/2509